20 FUN FACTS ABOUT BEAVERS

D1716256

BY CHARLIE LIGHT

Gareth Stevens
PUBLISHING

Please visit our website, www.garethstevens.com. For a free color catalog of all our high-quality books, call toll free 1-800-542-2595 or fax 1-877-542-2596.

Library of Congress Cataloging-in-Publication Data

Names: Light, Charlie, author.
Title: 20 fun facts about beavers / Charlie Light.
Other titles: Twenty fun facts about beavers
Description: New York : Gareth Stevens Publishing, [2021] | Series: Fun
   fact file: North American animals | Includes index.
Identifiers: LCCN 2019045636 | ISBN 9781538257623 (library binding) | ISBN
   9781538257609 (paperback) | ISBN 9781538257616 | ISBN 9781538257630
   (ebook)
Subjects: LCSH: Beavers–Juvenile literature.
Classification: LCC QL737.R632 L54 2021 | DDC 599.37–dc23
LC record available at https://lccn.loc.gov/2019045636

First Edition

Published in 2021 by
Gareth Stevens Publishing
111 East 14th Street, Suite 349
New York, NY 10003

Copyright © 2021 Gareth Stevens Publishing

Designer: Sarah Liddell
Editor: Kate Mikoley

Photo credits: Cover, p. 1 (main) Chase Dekker/Shutterstock.com; file folder used throughout David Smart/Shutterstock.com; binder clip used throughout luckyraccoon/Shutterstock.com; wood grain background used throughout ARENA Creative/Shutterstock.com; pp. 5, 6 (top) Christian Musat/Shutterstock.com; p. 6 (bottom) Podolnaya Elena/Shutterstock.com; p. 7 Stevenj/Wikimedia Commons; p. 8 Kamil Martinovsky/Shutterstock.com; p. 9 E Thomas/Shutterstock.com; p. 10 STORM INSIDE PHOTOGRAPHY/Shutterstock.com; p. 11 Elena Berd/Shutterstock.com; p. 12 Zadiraka Evgenii/Shutterstock.com; p. 13 Stan Tekiela Author/Naturalist/Wildlife Photographer/Moment/Getty Images; p. 14 karen crewe/Shutterstock.com; pp. 15, 20 Astrid Gast/Shutterstock.com; p. 16 SERGEI BRIK/Shutterstock.com; p. 17 Reimar/Shutterstock.com; p. 18 Danita Delmont/Shutterstock.com; p. 19 Geoffrey Kuchera/Shutterstock.com; p. 21 DEA/BIBLIOTECA AMBROSIANA/Contributor/De Agostini/Getty Images; p. 22 ian Tessier/Shutterstock.com; p. 23 PremaritalYolk/Wikimedia Commons; p. 24 SGeneralov/Shutterstock.com; p. 25 John Webster/Getty Images; p. 26 Ronnie Howard/Shutterstock.com; p. 27 higrace/Shutterstock.com; p. 29 UbjsP/Shutterstock.com.

Printed in the United States of America

Some of the images in this book illustrate individuals who are models. The depictions do not imply actual situations or events.

CPSIA compliance information: Batch #CS20GS: For further information contact Gareth Stevens, New York, New York at 1-800-542-2595.

Find us on

CONTENTS

Words in the glossary appear in **bold** type the first time they are used in the text.

NATURE'S BUILDERS

Have you ever heard the saying "busy as a beaver"? Maybe when you've been hard at work, someone has even called you an "**eager** beaver." Why are these cute critters known for being so hardworking? The answer is in their architecture, or how they build things.

Very few animals can change entire areas like beavers can. They build huge dams and homes called lodges. Plus, they even cut down trees to build with! Are you ready to meet these unbelievable builders? Read on!

Beavers are mammals, which means they are warm-blooded, have fur, give birth to live young, and mothers produce milk.

BIG BEAVERS

BEAVERS ARE THE SECOND BIGGEST RODENTS ON EARTH!

American beavers are the largest rodents in North America. Eurasian beavers live in Europe and Asia. They're the largest rodents where they live too. The only larger rodent alive is the capybara, which lives in South America.

NORTH AMERICAN BEAVER

EURASIAN BEAVER

The American beaver, *Castor canadensis*, and the Eurasian beaver, *Castor fiber*, are the only two species, or kinds, of modern-day beavers!

Castoroides was the largest rodent to ever live in North America.

EARLIER SPECIES OF AMERICAN BEAVERS WERE ABOUT THE SIZE OF A BLACK BEAR!

Castoroides was the **ancestor** of the modern-day American beaver. It was up to 8 feet (2.4 m) long and weighed about 200 pounds (91 kg)!

BEAVERS HAVE METAL IN THEIR TEETH!

There's a layer, or coating, on the outside of beaver teeth that's made of a lot of iron. This makes their teeth strong and keeps them from decaying, or rotting. It also gives beaver teeth a rusty orange color!

Scientists study the teeth of beavers and other rodents to learn how humans can take better care of our own teeth!

Beavers almost went **extinct** in North America because people hunted them for their fur. Millions of beavers were killed from the 1600s to the 1800s.

FUN FACT: 4

BEAVERS SECRETE BROWN SLIME FROM NEAR THEIR BUTTS!

This slime is called castoreum, and it comes out of **sacs** under a beaver's tail. Beavers leave their castoreum behind in places they live to mark their territory.

Beavers brush burrs, which are seeds with lots of sharp points, and **parasites** out of their fur.

BEAVERS HAVE A BUILT-IN COMB!

Beavers have front paws with digging claws. Their back feet are webbed, meaning there's skin connecting their toes that helps them swim. Each back foot also has one toe with a double nail. Beavers use these toes like a comb to brush their fur!

A BEAVER'S TEETH NEVER STOP GROWING

To stop their teeth from growing too long—and to keep them sharp—beavers chew on lots of wood. This is handy because they also need wood to build their dams and lodges!

A beaver can bring down a medium-sized tree in just one night!

BEAVER TAILS

BEAVERS HAVE A BUILT-IN MULTIPURPOSE TOOL—THEIR TAILS.

Beavers direct themselves with their tails while they swim. On land, they use their tails to help stay balanced while carrying heavy objects in their mouths. They even use their tails to sit up straight!

Beavers' tails are leathery and shaped like a paddle. They're also covered in scales!

Beaver tails can grow up to 18 inches (46 cm) long and 5 inches (13 cm) wide.

BEAVERS "TALK" TO EACH OTHER WITH THEIR TAILS!

If there's something scary around, beavers will hit their tails on water to make a loud sound. This noise warns other beavers that danger is near!

UNDERWATER ADAPTATIONS

BEAVERS CAN SEE WITH THEIR EYES CLOSED!

Beavers have an extra set of transparent, or see-through, eyelids. These eyelids work just like built-in goggles! They allow beavers to see underwater while protecting their eyeballs.

Beavers are built for a semiaquatic life, meaning they spend some of their time on land and some in water.

Beavers' underwater **adaptations** help keep them safe. Their lodges can only be entered by underwater tunnels, which can help keep predators from getting in.

BEAVERS CAN HOLD THEIR BREATH UNDERWATER FOR UP TO 15 MINUTES!

Beavers have special parts called valves in their nose, throat, and ears. The valves close when they go underwater. This keeps the water out!

BEAVER BEHAVIOR

BEAVERS KNOW HOW TO REFRIGERATE THEIR FOOD.

Unlike some animals, beavers don't spend the winter sleeping. They mostly stay in their lodge and eat the food they've stored on the bottom of their pond. The cold pond keeps the food fresh.

Beavers like to eat the same things they like to build with—trees and other plants! Some of their favorites are maple, birch, and willow.

16

Both males and females secrete castoreum oil on dirt piles they build around their territories. This is just one of many special behaviors, or ways beavers act.

BEAVERS' TERRITORIES MAY SMELL LIKE VANILLA!

The castoreum oil beavers secrete to mark their territories smells somewhat like vanilla! Castoreum is sometimes even used as a flavoring in food. However, it's hard to collect, so it's not used very often. Would you try it?

FAMILY LIFE

FUN FACT: 13

BEAVERS BUILD FAMILY GROUPS CALLED COLONIES.

Beaver pairs **mate** for life. They build their homes and raise their kits, or babies, together. Kits leave home at around 2 years old and find their own mates when they're about 3.

Beaver pairs are monogamous, which means they will only mate with each other. If a beaver's mate dies, it will find a new mate.

There can be anywhere from one to six beaver kits in a litter. When they turn a year old, they're called yearlings.

BEAVER KITS CAN SWIM WITHIN JUST 24 HOURS OF BEING BORN!

Beaver kits are born with their eyes open. After a few days, they're ready to explore beyond the lodge—they still stick with their parents for a while though.

19

BUSY BUILDERS

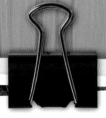

BEAVER DAMS CAN BE UP TO 10 FEET (3 M) TALL—THAT'S AS TALL AS A ONE-STORY HOUSE!

Beavers only grow to be around 3 feet (1 m) long, but their dams can be huge. The longest one on record is 2,790 feet (850 m)!

Beavers build their dams out of branches, baby trees, small tree trunks, and plants. They caulk, or seal, cracks with mud.

This drawing of a beaver dam is believed to be from around November 1866. Some dams that were mapped around 150 years ago are still in place!

FUN FACT: 16

SOME BEAVER DAMS ARE MORE THAN 1,000 YEARS OLD.

Scientists have found some really old beaver dams in California. There's one that they believe was built all the way back in the year 580!

BEAVER LODGES HAVE CHIMNEYS!

Beaver lodges are shaped like domes. This means they have big rounded roofs. They have a small hole at the top to let air in and out, so the beavers can breathe! This hole is called a chimney.

A beaver lodge can be 6.5 feet (2 m) tall and 39 feet (12 m) wide. Lodges are often built in the middle of ponds.

INSIDE A BEAVER'S HOME

CHIMNEY

LODGE

LIVING AREA

FLOOR

UNDERWATER ENTRANCES

The floor of the living area is usually covered in wood shavings, which soak up water. The beavers also use it as bedding to sleep on!

ECOSYSTEM ENGINEERS

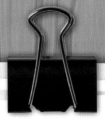

BEAVERS ENGINEER, OR CREATE, ENTIRE ECOSYSTEMS!

Some beavers build their dams on rivers. The dams raise some of the river water to create ponds where beavers build their lodges. These ponds make a wetland ecosystem where other plants and animals live too!

BEAVERS BUILD WETLANDS

WETLAND

RAISED WATER

BEAVER DAM

RIVER

Wetlands are ecosystems where water covers the soil or where the soil has a very high level of moisture for part or all of the year.

Although beaver dams sometimes flood, they can also help prevent flooding! Beavers have even been reintroduced, or returned, to some places in the world to limit floods.

FUN FACT: 19

BEAVERS SOMETIMES HAVE HARMFUL EFFECTS ON ECOSYSTEMS.

Beaver dams can cause flooding. This can destroy land people use for farming. It can also harm roads. Sometimes people put pipes in beaver dams to prevent floods.

BEAVERS ARE HELPING FIGHT CLIMATE CHANGE!

Beaver dams can also catch harmful matter, keeping the water cleaner.

The Methow Project moves beavers to places in the state of Washington that have limited amounts of water due to melting glaciers. The dams and ponds beavers create help keep water in the area.

27

LEAVE IT TO BEAVERS

People hunted beavers so much that in the 1800s they nearly went extinct. The good news is that people also helped bring these wonderful creatures back! After major **conservation** efforts, there's now a healthy number of beavers living in North America.

Beavers are a great example of what conservation can accomplish. We can help bring animal populations back, which can help keep whole ecosystems running. Beavers are a key part of their ecosystem—after all, every system needs its engineers!

Is there a beaver
conservation group near you?
Maybe you can start one!

GLOSSARY

adaptation: a change in a type of animal that makes it better able to live in its surroundings

ancestor: an animal that lived before others in its family tree

climate change: long-term changes in Earth's climate, caused partly by human activities such as burning oil and natural gas

conservation: the care of the natural world

eager: excited or interested

ecosystem: all the living things in an area

extinct: no longer living

mate: to come together to make babies. Also, one of two animals that come together to produce babies.

parasite: a living thing that lives in, on, or with another living thing and often harms it

rodent: a small, furry animal with large front teeth, such as a mouse or rat

sac: a bag-shaped body part

secrete: to produce and release

BOOKS

Patent, Dorothy Hinshaw. *At Home with the Beaver: The Story of a Keystone Species.* Berkeley, CA: Web of Life Children's Books, 2019.

Poliquin, Rachel. *Beavers.* Boston, MA: Houghton Mifflin Harcourt, 2018.

Romero, Libby. *Animal Architects.* Washington, DC: National Geographic Kids, 2019.

WEBSITES

DK Find Out: Beavers

www.dkfindout.com/us/animals-and-nature/rodents/beavers/

Learn more about how beavers build their dams with this interactive site!

National Geographic Kids: Beaver

kids.nationalgeographic.com/animals/mammals/beaver/

Click through an informative beaver slideshow and learn more about these amazing animals here!

PBS Learning Media: Beavers

ny.pbslearningmedia.org/resource/tdc02.sci.life.colt.beaver/beavers/

Watch this fascinating video about the amazing ways beavers can transform their environments!

INDEX